THE CARTOGRAPHER'S INK

Okla Elliott possesses a capacious mind that here integrates his complicated and informative personal geography, philosophical investigation, a touching lyricism, and an attractive sense of humor. The result is a brilliant collection about "the light here." The light is caustic with war, striated with love, sharply focused on our past, present, and future. "The Philosophy Student" persuades us that "[t] here is no convincing proof that we have any right to happiness," but because thinking actually occurs in his poems, they are tremendously exciting — and happy-making — to read.

—KELLY CHERRY, former poet laureate of Virginia and author of *Hazard and Prospect: New and Selected Poems*

"I wanted / the poetry of love // not the lowly prose /of inevitable and undeniable" writes Okla Elliott in *The Cartographer's Ink*. Seeking love and poetry, this impressive first book ranges across memory, history, geography, and philosophy with a wider imagination than any poet writing today. But it never gets lost in its erudition because the search for love and poetry becomes, in Elliott's hands, inevitable and undeniable.

—ANDREW HUDGINS, finalist for the National Book Award and the Pulitzer Prize

The Cartographer's Ink is a groundswell of "strange danger" where "the wet bloom of meat and bone" converge with Tesla, Newton, and Kierkegaard, while a few scenes over, the philosophy student takes on Chernobyl. Prepare yourself for journey-by-poet-pen battling the Humbaba, imbibing on the spirits of several dynasties, passing through the needle's eye with "Lines from Kim Ch'un-Su" and returning us to "World enough / Death enough / Applause for our many talents." Okla Elliott does not spare our sensitivities on any level. Like the embalmer's son, he will "dangle the corpse to drain." History, philosophy, and physics provide the landscape for adventure and interrogation alike; this journey in your hands, compressed trees and dusted ink by machine, evidences the human essence, "Want is a stone / shaped under this pressure."

—AMY KING, author of *Slaves Do These Things* and *I Want to Make You Safe*

What hunger there is in these poems! What powers of mind, yet a big heart as well, beating and beating. Wolves, Russian proverbs, an old woman in a Berlin flower shop whistling a song the poet doesn't know: anything and everything is fair game. Oh, and along the way, Okla Elliott pretty much reinvents the sestina—you try writing one that uses "icky" and "Solzhenitsyn" as end words.

—DAVID KIRBY, finalist for the National Book Award
and author of *The House on Boulevard St: New and Selected Poems*

Okla Elliott's work intersects poetry and philosophy—seamlessly and richly. *The Cartographer's Ink* reveals an original, moving voice. These are poems to be read and re-read and carried long in mind.

—STEPHEN KUUSISTO, author of *Letters to Borges*
and *Only Bread, Only Light*

The poems in Okla Elliott's debut volume, *The Cartographer's Ink*, chart—with linguistic dexterity and curious attentiveness—the intersecting geographical lines of space, time, and an always-already disintegrating self. Here, the poem is a three-dimensional map networking the fleeting yet nonetheless powerful personal ephemera of memory, emotion, and place (interwoven with cultural, familial, and erotic histories), onto an axis richly palimpsest with philosophical and scientific imagination. Elliott's poems zoom and slide through their various spectrums with exhilaratingly dizzying connect-the-dots that collide micro with macro—simultaneously paying homage to the immense and unlikely potential of intellect and imagination, yet never losing sight of the memento mori of the wine-filled skull, the quick and lovely sparks of a body soon to return to the cosmos.

—LEE ANN RORIPAUGH, winner of the
National Poetry Series and author of *Dandarians*

THE CARTOGRAPHER'S INK

Okla Elliott

NYQ Books™

The New York Quarterly Foundation, Inc.
New York, New York

NYQ Books™ is an imprint of The New York Quarterly Foundation, Inc.

The New York Quarterly Foundation, Inc.
P. O. Box 2015
Old Chelsea Station
New York, NY 10113

www.nyq.org

First Edition

Set in Book Antiqua

Layout and design by David Bowen

Cover image elements provided by and modified with permission from Struckdumb Graphics and naumoid/Bigstock.com

Author photo by Robert MacCready

Library of Congress Control Number: 2014945804

ISBN: 978-1-63045-010-6

ACKNOWLEDGMENTS

Birmingham Poetry Review: "Humbaba Clothed in Seven Cloaks"; "Tilting Toward Winter"

BLIP: Mississippi Review Online: "Lonely in Seoul"

Coe Review: "Emerging from Clouds"

Connotations Press: "Visiting Lenin's Tomb"

Contrary Magazine: "Alien War, Human War"

Del Sol Review: "The Parable of the Worm in the Apple"; "Shibboleth, Beginning and Ending with Lines from Kim Ch'un Su"

Fourth River: "Learning Russian"; "The Philosophy Student"

Fourth River: Best of the First Ten Years: "The Philosophy Student"

Freshwater: "What a Vulgar Moon"

Great Lakes Review: "The Artificial Suns of Milwaukee"

International Poetry Review: "A Hot Minute"; "Helpless"

The Laurel Review: "Pointless Movement"

The Literary Review: "That the Soul Discharges Her Passions Upon False Objects"

The Louisville Review: "Blackened"; "Nikola Tesla Dreams of a Death Ray Powered by the Forgotten Hopes of Angels"

The Los Angeles Review: "Wishing on a Shooting Star My Friend Informs Me Is Likely Just a Satellite"

Nashville Review: "Think of a House"

New York Quarterly: "How It Ended"; "The Man Who Named Bees"

Oyez Review: "Mannheim, Germany, Phone Booth in the Turkish District"

roger: a journal of the arts and literature: "Reading Kierkegaard Near the St. Louis Arch"; "Near the Ocean"; "The Light Here"; "Yardwork for my Dying Mother"

South Dakota Review: "The Unhappy Theatre"; "Wolf-Sense Sonnet"

The Southeast Review: "The Inside Bird"

Thin Air: "The Idiot's Faith"

Subtropics: "The Patience of the Landmine" (and reprinted as part of *Virginia Quarterly Review*'s InstaPoetry Series)

Zone 3: "On Perfection"

The following poems appeared in the limited edition chapbook *A Vulgar Geography* (MSR Press, 2011): "On Perfection"; "The Idiot's Faith"; "Near the Ocean"; "The Light Here"; "How It Ended"; "The Man Who Named Bees"; "Learning Russian"; "The Philosophy Student"; "Emerging from Clouds"; "Yardwork for my Dying Mother"; "Shibboleth, Beginning and Ending with Lines from Kim Ch'un-Su"; and the following poems appeared in the limited edition chapbook *Lucid Bodies and Other Poems* (MSR Press, 2006): "Lucid Bodies"; "What a Vulgar Moon."

In addition to thanking the editors at the above journals and presses, I would also like to thank the following people: Nancy Blake, for her unwavering belief. David Bowen, for years of friendship and for the design of this book. Raul Clement, for our many collaborations. Raymond Hammond, for his great work at NYQ Books and for selecting me to be part of the NYQ family. Andrew Hudgins, for his support and guidance. Brett Ashley Kaplan, for being the best dissertation director anyone could hope for. Sean Karns, for helping me with many of the poems in this book, and for his brave and unique vision. Kyle Minor, for our literary comradeship which has both pushed and sustained me. Cary Nelson, for three excellent poetry classes at the University of Illinois which inspired several of these poems. David R. Slavitt, for serving as a model and for leading me to write the poem "Humbaba Clothed in Seven Cloaks." Jillian Weise, for a million hours of poetry talk.

CONTENTS

I.

II.

III.

IV.

I.

THE LIGHT HERE

It sets a mood
of clownish tragedy,
of ecstatic failure waiting to happen.

It is not a static blue light
nor the throb of a strobe.

It is not a light to read by
nor to be naked in,
unless you are desperate
or barbarously horny.

I would use it to look for you
in a cave or catacomb
or an ossuary crowded by the famous dead —
that is, if you were in such a place,
I would use this light to find you.

It is a light that yellows the periphery.
It is not a light that brightens the center.

It is mixed from an overcast morning
and the electric urban dusk.

It is a light I could live in
if I came to terms with certain failings
in my character
and the character of others.

I know you have light where you are,
better light even,
but I wanted you to know
about the light here.

WOLF-SENSE SONNET

I will walk you through the desert, all wolf-
wolf and blood-sandy paws. O smooth rapture
of elegant neck — O underwear hanging
on comic cactus — water-plant, prick-plant
of need. I will lead you through strange danger,
one million nights of apocalyptic lust.
Gone giddy, I'll lick lasciviously
your Lilith lips, lunge, leap, and lie back down.

What am I saying? All sense has left me.
There's a zero at the bottom of this pit.
There's a note of desert music in us.
There's no need of sense, only our senses.

You will walk me wolfily into new need,
and our oasic images will mirror-mirage.

THE MAN WHO NAMED BEES

He named them
with the care
of a Parisian stamp collector.
One by one he named their bodies,
their wings,
memorized individual buzzes
unique as human voice
to those initiated in the delicate ways
of bees.

He gave them ancient names
— Prudentius, Avianus, Propertius —
the lesser Latin poets.

And at night, he slept
beside his wife,
whom he wanted to love
more generously.

IN THE DAYS OF NEW WONDER

Nikola Tesla watched a brown bear
climb the persimmon tree
and shake her snout
at the sour bites she took.
      He nursed
his sickness
by an open window,
seeing death in stellar signals.
        The brown bear
climbed down and gamboled
to Tesla's darkened frame and snorted
her animal displeasure.
           This is why
he did not sharpen the razor
purchased secondhand for loneliness.

This is how electricity made a home
in his disintegrating mind.

Near the Ocean

Why should the world laud
our sweetgrieved lives?

We swim our own silly graves —
lovely as a naked acrobat, spread out
for her mother's show.

                Near the ocean, in Argentina,
a woman I wanted to love me
                     — if only for that winter —
explained the mercy of waves, the mercilessness
of the rock wall.
           I asked *Do we drink the wave*
or the water? wanting to be profound,
which I have assumed women prefer.
She said *Neither, it is saltwater.*

We laughed but didn't have sex.

I walked to my small apartment —
the whole way pursued
by thoughts of drowning, by bricked alleyways,
the wicked taste of the ocean.

LONELY IN SEOUL

1.

Swift dog, come back. I know
your name in French, will read
the Korean newspaper
to you.
> But that isn't
enough. The dog is not impressed
by my learnèd posture.
He whines as he shits worms
and blood. He barks at death
and grins slobbery outside
empty storefronts.
> *Chien*
véloce . . . we might have been
essential friends.

2.

You can peel wet labels
from beer bottles
easier than wine bottles.
You can sleep longer if you
move to the futon at eight
a.m. and back to bed
at noon.
> I hear the food
is good but it doesn't
taste like anything.

3.

September is the month
for dancing wide-armed
in the Chu-Suk festival.
The women wear Han-Bok

dresses and sing along
with the high happy music.

I eat large meals, get drunk,
fall in love three times,
and return to the futon
for more sleep.

4.
Somewhere a man is drinking
cold water while he waits
for the woman he will marry.

Somewhere a sad boy pets
a slow dog lovingly.

Here the hands of foreign gods
press sleep into my mouth and eyes.

THE PATIENCE OF THE LANDMINE

Weeds grow over rusty death

in a field no crops

but many flowers

will populate. The landmine dreams

the sweetness of a child's foot

or a dog's paw to depress

its small detonator, dreams

the echoing boom

and the wet bloom of meat and bone.

It dreams its dream for years, decades,

does nothing but dream,

and never grows tired.

Humbaba Clothed in Seven Cloaks

"Why have you raised up my son Gilgamesh and
laid on him a restless heart that will not sleep?
Now you push him to go on a long journey to
the place of Humbaba, to face battle he cannot
understand and travel a road he cannot know…"

— *Gilgamesh* (John Gardner and John Maier
translation)

Gilgamesh calls out to us
warns of the unknowable he now knows
and of the battle with Humbaba
we are going to lose.

His seven cloaks
conceal his seven attributes.
He takes off one layer and slows,
revealing a further demise.

Humbaba's face of sickening eels,
his hatred fuller than the ocean.
The blood of his million million victims flows
in his brain as his own.

We will fight Humbaba, like those before.
We will fight, but our hopes
are empty arsenals.
We're meant to lose this war.

ALIEN WAR, HUMAN WAR

[*written on the tenth anniversary of the Iraq invasion*]

1.

Death is an underwater bird,
not a bird at all;
an eel with wings. It is a metal bird
loaded up with techno-artillery.

War, this war,
war between the eagle and other birds-of-prey
(different prey).

Death is depleted uranium,

radiating strangeness into the cells of our victims.
It is a strangeness we are all born into,
borne by all of us.

It is a strangeness taking many forms,
natural and un-
in equal measure.

Stranger still to be guilty
of murders we did not commit.

2.

Making ourselves alien to ourselves
we diminish all things.

That curve of a bell, the curve of buttocks
the bell-curve normalizing us all,
the image of a model's ass that makes us want
to find that image in the flesh of the world.

Making others alien to ourselves
we diminish all things.

The curve of a bell,
the curve of a missile scudding
toward its living targets —
the curve of a line representing
fatality statistics over a six-week period.

When an alien dies, nothing human is lost.
When we make others alien,
we diminish all beings.

3.

When the bird flies into the storm
it is gone to us. When the bird
swims into the earthquake
it is gone to us until   its perennial return.

4.

The imbricated self, the implicated subject.
The guilt-threads are tightly knotted.
Imbrication, implication — the nouns sound
so alien, so Latinate
I can't feel my way into their fact. Abstraction
alienates lived life. To make others alien
we must abstract them to mere ideas,
not particular flesh and thoughts peculiar
to them. To kill others we must   make them alien.

Murder, therefore, is an abstraction abstracted.

5.

Our appetites and terrors fill the gnawing void
of the world.

Our appetites and terrors fill the gnawing void
of the world.

Our appetites and terrors fill the...

LEARNING RUSSIAN (A LETTER TO MY SCHIZOPHRENIC MOTHER)

First, the exhausted smells of the city.
Then the snow. Then the words
for each. The sun rises

over Byzantine architecture; the morning
glints on gold and silver bulbs.

Stay where you are.

I feel the hugeness of Russia
in every Kaliningrad wind.

It's likely to snow all night.

And you, in Kentucky, in the house
where I was a boy,
and where you will die.

The sadness of the semi-ancient
Cyrillic letters.

Stay where I keep you.
You're not what you were.

Your skin loose, a sack
for your meat and blood.
Your smoke-torn lungs
failing more every day.

Stay where you are.
You're not what I keep of you.

Visiting Lenin's Tomb

1.

The mummy of Russia will not rise —

the mummy of Russia
with a woman's bullet still lodged
in his neck.

Russia is the home of the undead.

Any vampire would choose to live
in St. Petersburg
with its seventeen-hour nights.

And zombies crawl the clubs of Moscow
for black opium, funhouse-
mirroring the mummy
in his glass coffin.

2.

To be able to say finally
and honestly
that I want to live
in the time I am in, as the person
I am, with the facts and reasons
of myself broadcast all around me —

this, this —

is my single remaining dream.

3.

Russian proverb:
If you look into the terrible past,
you will lose an eye.
If you do not look into the terrible past,
you will lose both eyes.

4.

The slow pressure in his skull
bulged his eyes like turnips.

No revolutionary thoughts emerged
from his trauma-swollen brain.

BLACKENED

We entered the ice-coffined city
later than General Paulus had planned,
and found deserted houses,
the 122mm machine guns unmanned.

Winter had killed many of us
and blackened others' feet with frostbite,
flesh rotting to ulcerous bone.
All through the city, night

climbed from the ground — or so it seemed —
shadows lengthening
under trees and around corners. Wretched air
rose from the sewers, strengthening

our sense of dread. We huddled
in the garden and slept under
a death-black sky spitting black sleet.
In the distance, tanks rolled like slow thunder

on their hulking way to Stalingrad. *Defeat the name,*
you defeat the man, Herr Chancellor Schrank
insisted, and many of us believed him.
So we marched, afraid and cold, carried trunk

after trunk of supplies to reinforce our troops,
even as our feet froze blackly in our boots.

THE EMBALMER'S SON

The nobleman's innards form a jelly
in the godly jars. Myrrh is mixed, and stems
of cinnamon, where his lungs once sucked air.
Father delicately hooks into gray sponge
and tugs it round and out the nostril.

The jackal Tuamutef curls in lung-flesh.
Qebhsenuf settles in the fatty liver.
These are my father's gods, more powerful
than all the rest, for they make sweet passage
to the Land of the Dead.
                              But I don't care
for his or other gods. I would splatter
the noble sweetmeats to the floor. What does it
matter where dead men's gonads lie? I pour wine
into the skull, and dangle the corpse to drain.

THE NAME OF KNOWLEDGE

The Mexican anthropologist has made a find,
a career-maker.
But why now, so late in life?

Who can care about a career at this age?
he says out loud
to the books,
the artifacts, the dust that accrues in the life
of a successful-enough man.

When he was the invincible age
of twenty-two
he dreamed himself into university
boxed through opponents —
all in the name of human history,
the name of knowledge.

The bar-dogs loved him as one of them,
los profesores admired him,
envied his energy.

To have come so far.
(To have left so much distance unconquered.)

He has even known love —
all three kinds.

And what has it brought him to?

It is not joy — as it should be, as is his right —
but regret he feels.

He regrets the ignored red-then-blue spirit
of an old lover's need.

Regrets not heeding the menacing face
of an ancient Olmec god,
his pug-nose so like the sack
that holds a man's balls,
he thought when he saw it decades ago.

Regrets the thoughts counted in the millions
by their glittering non-destinations
and the fewer that met their lowly stations.
He sits in his study
smoking French tobacco, drinking Italian schnapps,
— oh, even now I will stay in character.
He sits
and he ponders two skulls:
the one on his desk, with its prehistoric secrets,
and that other one he has carried
with him everywhere.

Shibboleth, Beginning and Ending
with Lines from Kim Ch'un-Su

Now I will go with my flower eyes open . . .

My father's eyes and your wet eyes go with me,
angry dead and angry alive.

Like cracked brick, like pristine anarchy,
we sprawl on this carpet, my rough fingers
in your hair.
   Odd that we hope not to lose
or make life by our fucking.
     I'll go

to where my father's bright eyes lie dead,
and scream out nonsense — *swift dog! red car! cold day!*
You'll hear this and know it
as our shibboleth. You will speak it,
though not to me . . .
    I'm sorry . . .

I haven't answered your question.
      But lie here,
and I will lie here, on this green carpet.
We'll make our decision once it's too late.

. . . we are not filled with tears nor made of brass.

HELPLESS

Sejong the Great, fourth king of the Joseon Dynasty (15th century), hired scholars to create the Hangul alphabet because Chinese script, which the Korean aristocracy used for writing legal documents and poetry, was too difficult for mass literacy. He then composed the *Yongbi Eocheon Ga* ("Songs of Flying Dragons") in this new alphabet, as the vehicle for Koreans to learn their language and have a literature of their own. This is what I want to tell my friend when she says she has miscarried, but her body is still preparing for a birth, her stomach swelling with useless uterine fluids. "And I have these strange allergies," she says, "to bananas — and I fucking love bananas — and grass oils and green peppers." There's nothing to say and I know there's nothing to say and she knows there's nothing to say. But I tell her how the Hangul alphabet was invented and that there used to be politicians who wrote poems to teach their people the joys of literature. She cries and leans on me, and I don't let myself pull away when the helpless swell of her stomach presses against me.

LOUDLY LAUGHING GREEN

She enters the packed room in flimsy green

swaying sad with her woman's step.

The way it clings to such shape is pleasant

at first. I stare openly over a blue drink

as she bends to fill her small plate with sweet

gourmet cookies and pâtés. I'm happy

as a single man at one of these functions

can reasonably be. But soon

she's talking to that man and laughing,

placing her hand delicately

over her breasts, then moving that small hand

away. I'm drinking too many vodkas, and green

is all I can think: Slickest shiny green,

shapely green — loudly laughing green.

LUCID BODIES

> "And thus might the sun and fixed stars be formed,
> supposing the matter were of a lucid nature. But
> how the matter should divide itself into two sorts,
> and that part of it which is fit to compose a shining
> body should fall down into one mass and make a
> sun, and the rest is fit to compose an opaque body
> should coalesce, not into one great body, like the
> shining matter, but into many little ones; or if the
> sun at first were an opaque body like the planets, or
> the planets lucid bodies like the sun . . ."

> — *letter from Sir Isaac Newton*
> *to the Reverend Dr Richard Bentley*

1. *Toward a Coherent Theory of Lonely Bodies*

And thus are we divided:
into those who fall down and form a shining star
and those who coalesce into dark planets. Or:
the brightest among us began as dull glows
muffled under the soot of circumstance
until their fall-then-rise

      like the morning star . . .

Reverend Bentley asked Newton why all matter
didn't group together at the inside of the universe
if, as he'd proposed, every particle was attracted
to every other one.

With all that wanton attraction,
how could we not end up together?

Newton conceded that in a finite universe
this would be true, "but if the matter was evenly dispersed
throughout an infinite space, it could never convene
into one mass; but some would convene into
one mass, and some into another, so as to make an infinite
number of great masses, scattered at great distances
from one to another throughout all that infinite space."

And thus we cannot overcome the distances
between us, our attraction diminishing
at the inverse square of inconvenience.

But there are those who fall into lucidity,
and burn—a beacon for other lonely bodies.

2. *Rising from the Hardened Earth, a Prayer*

For the black sky bursts with pin pricks.

For there's a house without furniture.

For it was in this house the fish slipped into its dirty bath
  and learned to swim itself clean.

For not all of us were born gleaming
  but must fall and fall and stand back up against
  such great gravity.

For the lift of language is only enough
  for someone with nothing more tangible to call his own.

For who am I to question my better angels?

For they will always be right.

For who am I to question my worse angels?

They also bring me closer to you.

3. *The Charms of Soft Matter, Like the Old Chaos*

". . .this mass would affect the figure
of the whole space, provided it
were not soft, like the old chaos."

In childhood our faces bloom and burst
across the celestial canvas,
flowering against a black backdrop.

Predictable, though mysterious,
planets orbit and fight the greater
attractions of the sun, grand and lucid.

The opaque and the lucid masses
glissading toward an imaginary point,
wanting to collapse upon each other

to be taken in by such heavy arms,
turned into to something bigger
matter rewarded for its leaden charms.

A Hot Minute

What a strange phrase.
We'll stop by the bar for a hot minute, you say, or:
Talk with me for a hot minute.
As if what I had to say was so burning
a minute's explosion would release it all.
Or that the seats at our favorite bar were heated
beyond comfort, guaranteeing a brief stop,
not an elongating evening with a friend's
friends, whom we can't stand.
As if time itself suffered a feverish longing.
Or after the bar — as the stop signs
blur by like ambulances —
and I'm facedown on your front lawn,
my eyelids flame-red membranes,
you lean over me, coaxing,
and I paw at your breasts like a blinded bear.

WHERE MAN SITS ENTHRONED

The storm calls forth cold rain-ordnance
to wash the sands of the city of sand,
where whitegrain walls slow-melt away
by a million teardrops' acidtouch.
The city of sand is the voice
of mankind. The city of sand
is the shadow of a tired sun.
It's sand, just sand, sandsand. The storm
is Death come to ask forgiveness
in the begging tones of destruction
its holiness sets on mid-earth,
where man sits enthroned in sand,
in sandsand, in sandsandsand.

Mannheim, Germany, Phone Booth
in the Turkish District

Soot-film on the glass,
the pollution so thick in this city.

You call me, more than a dollar a minute
overseas, and we try not to think
about that or our last talk.

Now you're telling me about your father,
how his hair hasn't fallen out yet,
that your parents use condoms

because his semen would burn her.
I'd never thought of that
side-effect of chemo. You keep talking,

telling me about some dream you've had
(and written in your journal, no doubt,
thinking your dreams are colossally important).

I imagine the urgency they must feel—
the awkwardness, after so many years,
and the pure scientific wonder.

I ask why you called me, whether you think
this is a good idea, so soon.
You're the only one I could tell this, you say.

And I know I shouldn't, but I say,
Your phone bill will be awful.

How It Ended

She called to say
she was at her mother's
and the kids were with her

He looked at the blue ceramic vase
filled with purple and yellow blooms
whose names he didn't know

He listened to her voice
and wanted to ask
what sort of flowers these were

THE IDIOT'S FAITH

Three lanterns floated in the dream she told him, but he didn't
want to hear about lanterns. He wanted factories unbuilt,
windows smashed open. He wanted libertine wailings. She
denied being a builder of factories, but he knew her reputation.
A wind blew in from Montreal, or she said it was from Montreal,
said she could smell the bars of Rue St Laurent. He was skeptical
but didn't want to argue. What good are arguments on a
Saturday night? What good are arguments at all? She told him
again about her love of the French language, and he thought
maybe they were getting somewhere. The modern sunset outside
her window was spilled wine tinged with pollution. They went
down the mountain to town, found the trouble she had decided
they wanted. She called a homeless man a fallen Chinese god,
and they mourned his sad descent, forgetting (almost) their
own. That is the power of generosity, one use of our idiot faith in
human love.

THIS BOTHERSOME BIRD

Through the raw dawn
through the moist forest
our freezing gestures form.

A sunken light impoverishes
our Being-in-the-world.
But I linger, a slight gray bird
fluttering, chirp-chirping
at each flittering thought.

What would you do with me,
this bothersome bird?
The silent firmament is torn by my song.
From my clouded tower,
I survey the horizons of existence
and nonexistence.

You show me your nascent tenderness.
We teach each other the rudiments
of human kindness, my need
feeding your need to be needed.

Perch, please, with me on the edge
of an apocalypse. Let us open
our gray wings and prepare our flight,
two gray things disappearing
into the gray lighted distance.

II.

EMERGING FROM CLOUDS

We were younger.

In our small kitchen,
       steam from the goulash soup
       obscured you,
       wilted your image.

I thumbed through a German children's book,
Kinder im Wald.

This was before
the cobblestone sidewalks,

       the damp/cold smell
       of cathedrals,

before your first train ride
from the Frankfurt *Hauptbahnhof*
to soot-covered Mannheim,
where I taught English
to uneager students.

You'd never seen Europe
and had promised yourself as a girl
you'd marry a man
who'd take you.

       This was as close as you'd get
       to the fantasy.

I smelled the greasy, peppered air
       and wanted   exactly this.

I read to you,
      and you repeated each line.

"Der Schnee fällt langsam. Der Wald ist ganz weiss,"
      words mouthed slowly and fully,
      as though speaking to a lip reader.

"Dare shnie..." you began.
      "Der Schnee," I corrected.

"Dare shnay..."
      "...*fällt langsam.*"

"Dare shnay fellt longzam."

The wooden floors, a distinctly American feature,
      vibrate apart in my mind, like in a horror
      movie, light shining between the slats.

The fading varnish   the white specks
      from careless painters,
clanking radiators
      given life by boiled breath.
Freshly baked bread lay
on a tattered red   (faded to a chalky pink)
hand towel.

      Condensation clung to the wintry kitchen windows,
      and I drew an alpine range with my fingertip.

I had received my letter of acceptance
the previous day.
This meal was a belated celebration.

      (You had to work late shift at the restaurant,

so we postponed
until the following evening.)

That night as we went to bed
we turned the heat down
so we'd have to hug our bodies together
for warmth.

That night reminded me of nothing.
It was its own.

***

Her name was Lela Kittoìl,
        the Macedonian-born poet
I'd known
        before you and I met.

She was all bustle,
        electrified —
                I saw her as my
counterpart,
        but lacking my indecisiveness —

She refused to move to America,
and I had to return to complete my degree.

I admit now that I planned to see her,
innocently of course,
the first chance.

        (Please know I couldn't lie
        about any of this;
        it would be a waste

of our time.)

I did not intend for things to happen
as they did.

Though Lela and I ended our relations. . .

Hearts contradict themselves
and send us plummeting or soaring by turns.
But by now you know that.

Our single-room flat on *Leibnizstrasse*
was as great a pleasure to me as to you.

> The bakery with *Apfeltaschen*
> and *Käsebrötchen* you loved so much,
> the late-night sparks
> along the lines of the *Strassenbahn,*
> the hours of you reading the newspaper
> or children's books with
> dictionary (*Wörterbuch*) in hand.

I began and began a novel
I promised myself I'd write
during our year there.

"Everything is a Left Bank fairytale," you said.

Saturday mornings
> we walked to the *Marktplatz.*

Fresh mozzarella floated in milky water;
dirt-covered potatoes;
the skinless red-muscled goat's skull
with dead eyes staring

you swore you'd never forget. (Have you?)

All these completed our return
to the Old World of high culture.

I recall one night in particular:
   we were standing on a wrought iron bridge
   above a small stream in the park: the wavy reflection
   of a streetlamp shimmered spectrally
   on the surface, immune to the pull of the current:
     I reached
   under your dress and we raced home giddy as wolves.

***

Your favorite story from a collection
   (leather-bound, velvety yellowed pages)
of Norse folktales:

   The jester who convinced the king
   that the prince was the Devil in disguise
   and tricked him
   into beheading his own son.

   The king wanted to go down in history
   as the most righteous king,
   the king who had rid the world of the Devil.
   After the jester was gone,
     and the king realized what he'd done,
   he set himself the task of telling the story
   of how he'd killed his son
   for the rest of his life.

Then the trip to Freiburg.

I lied:
It was not for research purposes.

We were on the *Schnellzug* from Berlin to Paris.
When we got off in Freiburg
and watched it continue its journey,
we didn't know it would not arrive.

You made me promise to take you
to Paris and the Riviera.

The next day our stomachs sank
as we read headlines:
our train
had been derailed by terrorist pipe bombs.

We hiked in the *Schwarzwald*.
You asked why it was called that.
I answered
I didn't know
but thought it had to do with the bark
looking black.

The smell of browning leaves
and mushroom rot
made the air an extension of the earth.

We were aroused by travel,
but no place presented itself.

Next day I went to the toy museum alone.

I had arranged for Lela to meet me there.

Her husband, Herr Doktor Kowalski,

a moderately successful linguist,
was not invited.

We laughed at how we were
both married,
how time went by.

She showed me a poem
she'd written after I'd left:

> It's a slow story,
> a river of iron:
> this moving separate.
>
> Lives stick in blue sky
> cloud-dancing,
> plummeting some days.
>
> This trail of blood
> leading to the door
> entering and winding the stairs,
>
> is its own validation;
> it no longer needs us.
>
> We ride our flying horses
> and emerge from the clouds
> smiling, tear-stained.

(The translation is mine.)

I told her it was beautiful,
that its awkwardness
   I felt when I thought of her,
especially now.

I wondered if there was a hotel nearby
I could afford without your noticing.

Infidelity is made harder by limited funds.

We selected a dim restaurant for dinner.
Her hands pressed and rubbed
at my thighs and crotch so expertly,
with a knowledge of my sensitivities,
        they seemed to be my own.

When I returned that night,
I was bursting.
I assume you mistook my passion
as a continued symptom of travel's romance.

I'm sorry, though no apology can reduce what I've done.

***

That wasn't the only meeting Lela and I had.

During my office hours back in Mannheim
one week when she was able to escape Dr. Kowalski;
        another time, after a reading she gave in Heidelberg;
        and again, in the rank, cramped space
        of a train restroom.
                I should have confessed all this earlier,
        but it went on without incident,
        and I was able to convince myself
        that nothing wrong was happening.

I told myself—and believed
        (still do to this day),

the human heart has more room for love.
        But as we all agree,
                in action if not in words,
                the heart must be stifled;
                its wantonness is more
                than we are prepared to suffer.

***

Our year's end landed neatly on the seam
between spring
and summer   evicting us.

In the last week
you collected postcards
and took dozens of pictures
in a panic to remember daily things.

It was all a withering dreamworld,
a lost fictional landscape.

We boarded our plane,
and I decided then I'd have to tell you,
though I knew

        the way you would have to go back
        and reinterpret every event, step
        by step,
        removing the sheen,
        replacing it with the dirt of lowly facts.

"We were younger," I said
        as the plane, descending,
                pierced the thinnest layer of cloud.

III.

TILTING TOWARD WINTER

The air is gray and quiet as the sea's
wet-dying warmth. A blackbird
screams out from memory and, pleased
with its sour chirping, keeps at it undeterred
by the browning season. I have everything
I could wish for—this air, this sea, this night.
We tilt toward winter, though the sand is spring
sand, erotic and youthful. Spirits are light
as May lasciviousness. But blood swells
to shore in cool disintegrating waves—
gone summer and gone winter aren't real.
I walk into the unwarm froth, say farewell
to my selves that have died and pray for those still
to die—their wet wombs, their thick-salt graves.

Nikola Tesla's Dream of a Death Ray
Powered by the Forgotten Wishes of Angels

He worked alone with X-rays, hour on hour,
forgot to sleep for days and then collapsed.
10,000 planes flew mute and languid through
pink Serbian clouds. A black ray swept
across their path, and they vanished as souls
floated Northwest toward oblivion.
The angels laughed at Tesla lying cold.
His want to wake was strange, he thought, in dream
lucid as if he had consumed two pots
of strong tea rapidly. This new invention
would dog him, just now when he had no time
for death rays. What would power it?, he wondered,
as he swam the pond behind his father's
parish where he preached a god so strange
as to conceive of matter, force, currents,
gravity, and microwaves. Wishes
of angels. This would be the power source
for his death ray. Forgotten ones, the most deadly.

He woke
              and lifted himself.
                              Saliva stuck

to his dry lips.
              He cringed, remembering

angels, and dipped his hands and dunked his head

into the washbasin.
                              Drops scudded down

his spine—
              as he saw planes in flames, smelled death.

Machine-Minded

Sludge gathers in the corners.
Clunk-clank the mind thinks and thinks
through each insoluble problem. A frantic heat
emanates in every direction. The perennial ache
ripples the surface of consciousness;
a forgotten loss stalks the depths.
Loss is a pit where the self can fall
and fall. Machine-minded,
it overcomes obstacles with solid routine.
It has learned to worry in the right ways.
It has learned many useful tricks for integration.
There is the matter of will and of self-illusion.
Oil gathers, congeals, encases the mind.
The thoughts are good thoughts,
crisp and almost one's own.
The thoughts rush forward
and disappear in the sludge at the edges.

WHAT LONELY CONTINENTS

Last night I dreamt of Africa it was beautiful and strange but you
weren't there and that made things more difficult even in the
unreality of dream made me think Africa really is a desolate place
worthy of all our pity how could a continent survive without
you I thought and realized Europe suffered the same poverty
of you and so was no better than Africa which at least made
me happy not to be dreaming I was in Europe but no happier
I was dreaming of Africa where the lions yawned with regal
indifference the gazelles ran languid with fear and slower than
in real life they were sad not to have you there and ran slower
thinking maybe you couldn't catch up that's why you weren't
but they were just dumb gazelles hoping against reason that you
wanted to be but just couldn't which is bullshit as you and I both
know try telling that to those stupid gazelles though they won't
listen to a word just run lazily along hoping you'll arrive just in
time to save them.

AN ARCHIPELAGO OF RAINBOWS

I show you a man walking, unharried,
unhurried. He is perhaps on his way
to visit a beautiful woman, or a woman
of average attractiveness, or an ugly woman
he nonetheless feels animal lust for.
Let's make it this last option,
because I like it better.

So this ugly woman is a philosophy student,
and the man is an accountant
of slightly above-average handsomeness.
They are not wealthy and they are not poor.

The man feels a perplexing enthusiasm
as a tip-toer through the abyss,
clownish juggler of desperations and desires.

He heats the flowers in boiling oil.
He crushes them with a stained wooden spoon.
He mashes and mashes, making a hot colorful pulp.

She looks at him, after sex, with her limpid eyes
and does not say, though she thinks, *Our brevity
refracts across the day.*

Just moments before it was thrust, thrust,
thrust. O you cannot imagine
how much they enjoyed sex together—
or maybe you can. I hope so.
(For your sake and for the sake of my poem.)

He walked casually naked to the bathroom
that sensitive pendulum wilted with satisfaction.

He was a July man, she a September woman,
but they were finding ways to make it work.

There had been storms all week, and the water
everywhere was rising dangerously.
They stood on her small balcony
(a feature he loved about her apartment
but never told her) and watched the riverbed
widen, threatening
to wash the whole lovely landscape away
and leave them alone, with nothing.

Pointless Movement

Everything had gone wretchedly backwards
at home and in the world. This pointless movement
of hands pleading like trapped birds,
breaking free, trapped again in a muck of desire.
I added more mire to their grave.
Hey, I pretended I said, *you owe me your despoiled blood.*
Such imagined dialogue was often my sinking
point of departure
at that time in our lives.
You are my brazen pomegranate, I didn't say, *more enticing
than any worm-tunneled apple of myth.*
Your silence was bogus. My silence — no, I owned no silence,
but I was bogus nonetheless.
Our patterned selves, playing at being ourselves,
non-coextensive concepts — me and I, you and you.
The canopy of our consciousness streaked by jet-streams, often.
I checked my watch,
but the time kept changing.
Amorous spirits, we pursued our selves,
but sometimes we got lost, forgot us,
became scattered puzzle pieces.
We stopped to populate our histories and futures,
suturing each to each, fertile with bizarre need.
I would marry you, I didn't say.
I drink my coffee your way now, I didn't say, *to be closer with you.*
Pointless movement, pointless. But I do it anyway.
A part of your spirit, a tiny part,
was in the way you drank beverages,
the way you ate, walked, held your cellphone
with shoulder and tilted head.
You owe me nothing, okay? I didn't say. *You have built me bigger
with the parts of your self you've left behind.*
I am aflood with you-patterns, a gift from our time,
from utopia to apocalypse.

STARS OF ORION

1.
The wet slope of the grassy hill and a blackbird.

Gas fumes and a sad song on the radio.

Sweat on my back and your careless v-neck.

Squawking birds flying in a sideways V.

After the burying, your head in my lap

for hours through Nebraska. Lying in a field

at four in the morning.

2.
If we had not seen so many flashes of road
If we had not seen ourselves at night
If we had not seen our parents dying
If we had not loved and not loved
If we had not enjoyed small cruelties
If we had not been born

3.

Scattered	the seeds	the seeds
Scared	we	we
Alive	the seeds	we
Time	murderers	scared

The seeds   dead   buried

We   murderers   scattered

4.

Stars of Orion and the clouds

of New Mexico. Washing blood

from the car and singing. You say we should

buy a burro and we laugh.

I say we should buy a unicorn

but we don't laugh. We look for the Pleiades

but don't find them. Too tired to fuck, we sleep

on the hood of the car.

THE ARTIFICIAL SUNS OF MILWAUKEE

1.

The summer city was hatching
cars along the water's edge.
Their lights went on,
slicing visible the Milwaukee night

as the lyric graywater
of Lake Michigan
flowed around the prose of fact.

Ten dollars a ticket
and we bicycle-pedaled
a romantic boat. Ripples bent
against the boat's tip.

Which facts? you asked.
Your bleared features glowed flesh-colored
in the headlights' light.

Now? I said.
You want to talk about this now?
I pedaled harder,
paddling the boat onward.

I could not illuminate
the facts. I wanted
the poetry of love,

not the lowly prose
of inevitable and undeniable.

2.

I loved the January wind;
I wanted unplanned intensities.
Sick dizzy snowflakes

careened toward our backs.
Blood-chilling lacerations of January.
Two mammals, we curled
in a snarling half-darkness lit

by streetlamps along Locust Street. Curled together,
wrapped in brocaded quilt, panes shivering
against the frame. The old facts overcome,

we steered our sleep through the bending night.
We breathed our mammalian love.

3.

Poetry wants too little, you said.
No, too much, I argued.
It pretends to want too much, you said, *but really*

it wishes it were a novella by John O'Hara.
We were reading,
bedside lamp angled down on us,
and I wondered if there could be

a John O'Hara of Milwaukee. Milwaukee
needs one, I decided. And I decided
I would become the John O'Hara of Milwaukee.

Next door, the neighbors were arguing,
and I regretted every cruel thing I ever said to you.

4.

Today, the pavement reminds me of a womb—
the whole city, its warm solidity.
It reminds me of a gas chamber, an exercise facility,

an alien landscape. It is comforting.
First, the exhausted smells of Milwaukee.
Then the reflected sunlight. Then the words.
Gasoline fumes and a sad song on the radio.

Sweat on my back; your careless v-neck.
Squawking grouses flying in a sideways V
over the lake. Locust Street is a text,

vagrantly composed. I read our poetry
into the prose of every avenue.

THE PHILOSOPHY STUDENT

Oksana remembers the stories about her grandfather being ordered by his Soviet bosses to clear out the forests and cities near Chernobyl. He used his soldier's rifle to shoot potentially contaminated animals, chopped them apart with an axe, doused them in gasoline, and burned them to nothing. He shoveled up grass, poured tons of sand on the ground, crowbarred wooden shacks apart. She remembers this now, standing outside her brother's bedroom door, imagining herself naked with his friend who is sleeping. He stopped by on his way to the Chechnyan front; her brother is already there. She is standing in the hallway, imagining herself naked, imagining this boy with his soldier's muscles as she reaches down and rubs her clitoris. But she stops, losing all interest—in the boy, her country's history, life itself. *There is no convincing proof that we have any right to happiness*, she thinks and walks down the hallway to her room, where at her desk she will continue her studies.

THE UNHAPPY THEATRE

In the courtyard, the leaves
wear sunlight like make up.
Cerulean warblers sing
extinction songs
and become blue-feathered actors
in my spring orgy.

The largest one is King of the Maple;
the smallest is the endangered dauphin
whose love for his twittering
sister-in-law is widely seen
as inappropriate.

Hissing squirrels hop branch
to branch, merrily chasing
each other's genitals.

But I refuse the sympathies of nature,
refuse the beauty of happy girls.
I will sit here until the birds
are dead and sex a memory

like the smell of the old woman
I saw in a Berlin flower shop
whistling a song
I did not know.

APOCALYPSE AND ABUNDANCE

All the ghosts of the house had taken the day off.
The neighborhood's chattering was shuttered upon itself.

We decided to open the lusty door of tomorrow, decided
        to make the tumult of flesh manifest.

We erased our quivering corpses. We drank bitter rum
        and laughed in a paroxysm of awe.

You said time is a tender pendulum. You said sex is a portent
        of nothing but itself. I disagreed but stayed silent.

You made stockinged progress across the carpet.

The fine olive curve of your hip was perfect.
Your tangled hair jutting many directions reminded me
        of the seven arms of the candelabra, of apocalypse
        and abundance.

I followed to the bathroom and watched with blunt happiness
        as you corrected the tilt of a mirror.

KALININGRAD

In Kaliningrad Natalie asks
whether I love her,
and though I might, it seems odd
to ask here.
               Fifty miles north,
the skeletons of WWII soldiers lie buried
under the beach. You can dig up a knucklebone
and bring it home with you, a souvenir.
Prostitutes stand in front of run-down government
buildings, cubes of Soviet concrete, or at the shipyards
rusted with disuse.
               "Why do you ask?" I ask.
We're eating pashtet, which I've never had before
and don't like.
Natalie sets her hand on mine and says,
"I just needed to know."

THINK OF A HOUSE

1.

By day it looks like a bad painting,
pure kitsch—the sky-blue backdrop,
green tobacco swaying in the field,
two dogwoods in bloom at each end.
It is summer now,
but if you were the son who lives in this house,
you would remember last winter
when the cedar fenceposts wore skullcaps
of snow, and the yard was punctuated
with three-footed rabbit tracks.

2.

The father doesn't drink, but he used to.
The mother isn't happy, but she was
and wonders if she will be again.
One daughter is smart, the other pretty,
and both believe the pretty one will always win.
The son, who is the youngest, thirteen,
memorizes verses from the Book of Isaiah
—*enter into the rock, and hide thee in the dust*—
and listens in the woods
for what he calls God's yodel. If he hears it,
he has no idea what he'll do.

3.

A story about the family might prove helpful:
Once there were pork chops and gravy and sweet corn.
The son ran through the kitchen,
and the smart daughter, who was also mean
with the curiosity of smart girls, tipped the pot
of boiling water onto him.
It was called an accident, but the son knew.

He glared at the smart daughter as he chewed,
pressing the icepack his father gave him
against his scalded arm.

                    4.
Another: When the pretty daughter was fourteen,
she sat in the father's lap, but he told her to get down.
She hadn't felt his erection, and so was confused
and hurt. (And what's worse,
the father hasn't so much as hugged
his pretty daughter since.)
The mother had always favored the smart daughter
while the father favored the pretty one,
but after that day,
the pretty daughter was on her own.

                    5.
Let's look at the house at nighttime.
Insects do their insect business.
The dogwoods blossom a ghostly gray.
The blue curtains make the windows glow blue.
We hear the murmur and see the flicker.
We see shadow-figures going room to room.
Let's make it a clear night, the sky bursting
with white pinpricks.
And there's the son, coming out on the porch
to piss, tired of waiting on his mother
who has been in the shower for over an hour.
He looks across the field
to the neighbors' house and says,
as though everyone in the world should hear him,
Therefore with joy shall ye draw forth water from the wells.

YARD WORK FOR MY DYING MOTHER

The mower drones, a hornet swarm

or lion humming the faithless tune

of battle hymns.

I'm tired, want nothing

more than sleep, but the lawn's grass blurs

in green defiance. Why keep growing?

The flimsy red machine spits

and fumes as I aim its stained blades

over an ant mound and enjoy

my petty genocide.

The book

of graying sky reads rain and flash.

The bodies will wash away

in sandy runnels, become scattered

chapter and verse on my mother's lawn,

where I await death's bulging arms.

NIGHTFISHING

By the beam of a plastic flashlight,
I saw the torn shadow
of a carp flopping hard against
the boat's metal bottom, as the radio

whizzed a worn tape of The Rolling Stones
made high-pitched and tinny by cheap
speakers. The fish's shimmery death
and its wet-smacking body seep

in, rise up in watery memory.
I stopped childhood
to wonder about the souls of fish,
my hands and clothes covered with mud.

Then later, home again, I heard
my father's cough cracking phlegm
in the wetness of his chest, and I knew
we're all fish inside, that life would take him

swift as the final crack
of a fish's head on thin aluminum.
And one day, I knew, I'd be that fish,
choking on a breath that will not come.

WHAT A VULGAR MOON

A boy studies the strangely
three-footed rabbit tracks,
tries to reproduce them
with his gloved thumb,
forefinger, middle — or,

another winter,
the three shallow holes
and blood in their center.
He followed, crashing excited
across an awkward field.

The snow lay dully, lethal white
against the moon's gray glowing

until he saw the thing,
its face torn off
        — one eye hanging.

The guilt.
That it was his fault
because he was so eager to hunt,
though he didn't know
what that meant.

But now he isn't thinking of that winter.
He is trying to emulate
the lightness of the rabbit's gait,
the way it moves so fast
that two of its feet
merge into one.

Entrances and Exits

When I was a younger man, a boy,
the intrigue of washing machine doors

trunks, windows, manholes — secret passages
of all sorts — possessed me. I spent hours

passing through and back through
a simple hole in the wall of a condemned house

careful to step with the other foot
or at a new angle each time,

conducting experiments that might foretell
how the world would receive me

and how I would leave.

IV.

READING KIERKEGAARD NEAR THE ST. LOUIS ARCH

"I shall certainly attend your party, but I must make
an exception for the contingency that a roof tile
happens to blow down and kill me; for in that case,
I cannot attend."

— Søren Kierkegaard, *Concluding
Unscientific Postscript to Philosophical
Fragments*

1.

The sky is oily blue and cool
as I imagine Copenhagen
was a hundred and fifty years
ago.
    St. Louis is peopled
with unlike demons firing pink
the sky with late sunset dying —
the river fired with city lights.
Above it all, the Arch, a sign
canting majestic low-high-low,
suggests a mirrored possible
subterranean self that doesn't
exist except in the small meta-
physical sense of being
imagined and needed by me.

And so: 2.

If all these abstractions detract
by being real only in ersatz
realities, then lead us not
into concretion. What rots
firmament cracks the fundament.

Therefore: 3.
The blackbird flies through the Arch
and flies with the Missouri River
beyond my vision 'til white stars
are washed with my seeing, made real-
er by my seeing them and not
seeing the blackbird which will fly
until it finds another rest.

It is time to go to the party,
and I will go, unless of course . . .
But no, not tonight—my canted
imagining is with me now.

On Perfection

1.

My arrogance is perfect —
I want everything I say taken down
in italics. I want
footnotes longer than the original text.
Every woman and many men
will want to look into the green almond eye
of my perversion.
                    They will thank me
for the privilege of disinterested touch.

I claim to be made of starstuff
brought here across a million million miles.

I claim to be happy
in the inevitable loneliness.

2.

The sanctified blade is perfect.

The colossal slowness of dying is perfect.

Everything is exactly as it should be
here where a goat's shit glistens with the water
of an idyllic river
he drank at hours ago,
hydrating his living (and dying) cells.

I have become a mystic
                    a perfect destiny
after all these years
                    of studied incredulity.

The unsanctified flesh is perfect,
I tell you,
because it always-already knew
every kind of love
our holy pornographers pretend
they invented.

3.
The slick tongue of metaphysics
flicks between stained teeth.

A tongue that could wet
dry lips or give a lecture
on Wittgenstein or lick the needy
flesh we hide (stupidly)
most of the enormous time we have.

4.
The spindle pricks the thumb wants
the needle.

A vest of goldthread
should be buried
with the dead.

Everything will rhyme
in the afterlife
as it does in the beforedeath.
It's as I've
said: perfection permeates
the sound fundament
and the cracked firmament.

It's as I've said, *tsk tsk*,
it's perfect
just as it is.

The feast prepares itself.

I Want to Be a Buddhist — Or: Reading Martin Heidegger Mildly Hung-over

The silver is responsible for the chalice is responsible
for the sacrificial vessel.
There is a wheel. There are two wheels —
the small wheel and the great wheel.

After a night of whiskey celebration,
a watery sense of hilarity washes over everything.
I want to leave the filthy world behind.
I want to be a Buddhist but can't
because it seems like an affectation.
I don't want to be seen as a person who harbors affectations.
That is to say, I am too attached to my image in the world
to become a Buddhist.
But if I was a Buddhist, I could maybe overcome my attachment
to my image and to the World.

I want to be a Buddhist but can't because I like whiskey
more than enlightenment.

Also, I can't give up my ambitions.
I work with an icepick's intuition.
I know Aristotle's four causes; I know the horizon of my Being.
I have known bad faith and good. I want to want
to be a Buddhist.
I have felt the green energy that erects life, the earthly pulse
that wobbles us all upright.

I want want want and want
and therefore am a failed Buddhist.
My ambition is to be a Buddhist.
Buddhist ambition is my new favorite oxymoron
(not that I had an old favorite oxymoron).

But what if this secular mysticism, this existential awe,
this wanting to be a Buddhist makes me a Buddhist?
The ice crashes loud and slippery,
melts to hilarity.
      Hilarity is the world withdrawing from me, me
detaching myself from the world, like a proper Buddhist.

The silver is responsible for the chalice is responsible
for the empty vessel. There are two wheels — one great,
one small.

THE PARABLE OF THE WORM IN THE APPLE

Resistant red skin
when fresh and undented —
the worm smushes its headless mouth
futilely against.

But weather wears softness into the flesh
till push-mouthing gets Willie Worm in
the serpent's globe. (Or is it Eve's? God's?) No one's
watching as Willie works all this while,
worried in his wormy way
a bird will snatch him by his ass-less other end
and eat him up (*chirpity-chirp!*).

But the gods of burrowing — worshipped also by mole
and centipede — smile their dirt-y smiles
upon our hero. He is in
an infinite heaven, a buffet without end.

And Willie has a message
for uptight philosophers with rules like Kant
and for uptight lovers who want to let go but can't:

When the worm in the apple has feasted
the apple is in the worm.

Sestina for the Swede-Nevadan

— *for Emilia Snyder*

Sometimes this place makes a girl feel plain icky,
no other word for it, sitting at the bar with a purple
martini. Makes her wish there was some ointment
to warm a Nevadan heart in Ohio's blizzard.
It also makes her want a chainsaw
to cut her way free, like a character from Solzhenitsyn.

And you have to wonder what Solzhenitsyn
would make of this stylish crowd. They're sickly
soldiers, chattering unpleasant as a chainsaw.
But if he read her stories, saw her skill,
I bet he'd forget about those hard Siberian blizzards.
The words would be like ointment.

But how does she make this ointment?
What are the ingredients? Start with one part Solzhenitsyn,
then add some Marquez, and stir like a *Blizzard
of One*. Reading it can be a bit tricky —
you never know when to stop clapping, your face gone purple
with laughing. The prose tears along like a chainsaw.

But what happens when the chainsaw
sputters, breaks down? What kind of ointment
is needed? She says, "My prose has gone purple!"
"Who knows?" I say. "Maybe read some Solzhenitsyn."
But my advice doesn't make her feel less icky.
The words float meaningless, like flakes in a blizzard.

Finding the way back is harder than unicycling in a blizzard
or juggling two hairless cats and a flaming chainsaw.
Oh, why must we sometimes feel so damned icky?

And even the artist's ink can't serve as ointment.
We have to wonder if the greats—Tolstoy or Solzhenitsyn—
ever felt so silly (yet so serious) a dilemma, looking into purple

horizons behind The Bronze Horseman, its skin gone purple
and gray with verdigris. Their magnificent blizzards
in Russia were punctuated, I'm sure even for Solzhenitsyn,
by a wish for clowns with seltzer and chainsaw
to cure a silly-serious ailment with a silly-serious ointment.
I guess what I'm saying is: Even the greats sometimes felt icky.

So pull out your chainsaw and carve from the icky
feeling a blizzard of prose and, like Solzhenitsyn,
drink your vodka (even if it's purple) as anodyne and ointment.

WISHING ON A SHOOTING STAR MY FRIEND INFORMS ME IS LIKELY JUST A SATELLITE

> "God in the beginning formed matter in solid,
> massy, hard, impenetrable, movable particles,
> of such sizes and figures, and with such other
> properties, and in such proportion to space, as
> most conduced to the end for which he formed
> them."

— Newton, *Opticks* (1704)

1. *(Ha-ha.)*

But isn't it the wishing that matters
more than the celestial talisman?

To what purpose did God make our wishing
for things we'd probably be better off without
(assuming for the sake of this poem
that we believe in Newton's God)?

And (be honest now)
aren't those hunks of telecommunicational metal
orbiting the Earth — the wet dream
of some sci-fi author from the fifties —
just as miraculous as stars?

More so, I'd say.
A bunch of burr-haired, shit-smeared apes
tossed those things up in space
sending radio waves and pornographic images
to the dorm room of a lonely college boy
whose ex-girlfriend will not answer
her cell phone, no matter how many times he calls.

The crowning achievement
of the animal kingdom. (Ha-ha.)

I'm sorry. This is getting us nowhere.

2. *This Poem Is for My Friend*

This poem is for all the mice in the hedgerow
            quivering at the scent of the farm cat.

It is for the boy born blind
            and the one with leukemia who won't
            get his three score and ten
            like the Bible promised.

This poem is for Isaac Newton
            who spent nearly a decade in
            a state of nervous collapse
            and never married.

This poem is for me.

But mostly it's for that lonely bastard
            calling a girl
            and for the fifties geek
            who would've done the same,
            if only cell phones
            had been invented then.

It is also for my friend
            who exploded my momentary
            and non-committal belief
            in the luck of shooting stars.

Thanks a bunch, asshole.

3. *On the Zodiacal Powers of Satellites*

We don't yet understand
the zodiacal powers of satellites
and blinking night-time jetliners,

though I believe they will
lead us to as strange a messiah
as some distant supernova did
two thousand odd years ago.

Like everything in our inventive history,
it'll start as a whisper
then grow to either a symphony
or a ballistics test.

They are vessels designed to bring us closer,
the gravity of communication between countries,
like the other day when

I was talking to a girl I dated in Germany
(who does answer her phone).
Just by hearing her voice
I decided to get a second job
so I could afford airfare.

It can be like that, these artificial signs —
read into them whatever you want.
It doesn't matter.

And that's what I've been trying to tell
my friend all night, but he insists
I'm writing this poem to prove a point
I don't even believe.

THAT THE SOUL DISCHARGES HER PASSION
UPON FALSE OBJECTS

> "...the amorous part that is in us, for want of a
> legitimate object, rather than lie idle, does after
> that manner forge and create one false and
> frivolous."

> — *from Montaigne's essay with more or
> less the same title as this poem*

Montaigne tells us, *Man (in good earnest) is a marvelously vain,*
    fickle, and unstable subject, and that seems about right,
though I don't know why I should be thinking of Montaigne
    just now, as I search for movies on Netflix,
where I am deciding between a foreign film or a cartoon,
    but an adult one, like Fritz the Cat, with its cartoon magpies
playing jazz — and by the blackness of their feathers
    and the blackness of their music we're meant
to know that these are black men, not magpies,
    or not really magpies but metaphorical magpies,
and that the segregation of species is wrong,
    that these magpies are real cool cats (ha, get it?),
but there's a problem with this, the idea
    that different species can represent different human races
because we're all one species, and so, as someone
    like Judith Butler or Slavoj Žižek might say, the act
of critiquing race relations actually reinforces
    the racist ideological assumptions about the differences
between the races, and they'd be right to say that,
    but when I was twelve and living in Argyle, Kentucky,
watching Fritz the Cat with Trace Reams I thought I was seeing
    something (and therefore being someone) very profound.

I thought about human equality and freedom
    and about whether I could sneak back into the movie room
later to watch the R-rated cartoon Heavy Metal
    to which I had masturbated once, which was only maybe
the second or third time I'd ever done that,
    and so like a boy who grows attached to his first lover,
I felt the heroine of this cartoon was necessary
    for me, nevermind that she had purple hair and flew
a reptilian creature and chopped people to bits
    with a massive sword — none of that mattered since she wore
leather lingerie while she did all her flying and killing,
    and she had matching purple nipples which were shown
several times. And so I make my Netflix decision.
I'll watch Heavy Metal and see what twenty years have done
to it and me. I half-wonder if I'll end up jerking off to a cartoon,
    which was forgivable twenty years ago but would be a
mixture of pathetic, deviant, and just plain sad now,
    especially with me thinking of Montaigne for no good reason
and unable to find a way to bring all this back around to his point
    so that my poem can have a satisfying end — an end that closes
the hermeneutic circle like we expect from poems.

The Apocalypso — Or: May I Have the Last Dance?

He wears slick black slacks and an overcoat,
boot polish glistens on fancy dancing shoes.
A darkling prince, a platinum noose.

His lips red and thick,
he savors the grease of his every meal.
Devours girls and boys alike. O how they squeal.
His angel-white Sunday shirt fluid-flecked
and in worrisome disarray.

He sees the world with children's eyes, stolen
from their bobbling heads. Light streaks bright and golden.
It is wrong to call him evil. He will play
his tune through this jaunty apocalypse.

He grins at the sun's darkening eclipse.
Look, look at the lovely grease on his lips.

The Inside Bird

My friends of the broken window
I beg you for patience

There will be night enough

There will be deeds
we will wish to forget

World enough
Death enough

Applause for our many talents
we have refined with self-love
for years, decades, waiting
for this applause
which sounds different than expected

But the glass jags threateningly
Eyes are vulnerable globes,
hands fleshy spiders skittering

There is a fallen bird
on both sides of the window

The outside bird is a cardinal, dead
The inside bird is actually a bat

My friends of the broken window
let us nurse this inside bird
to screeching health
                    Let us make its future our own

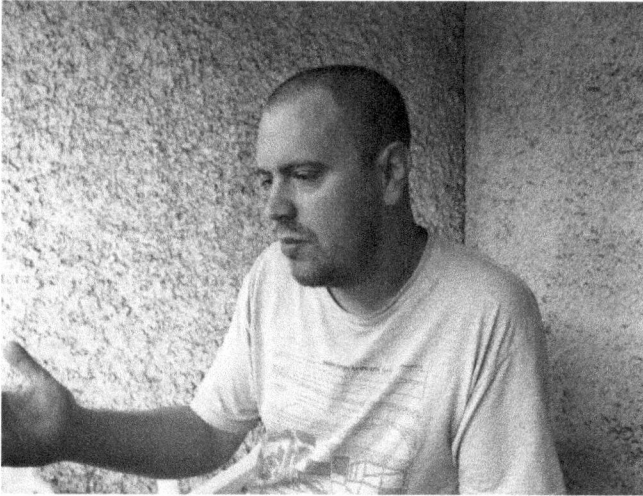

OKLA ELLIOTT is an Illinois Distinguished Fellow at the University of Illinois where he works in the fields of comparative literature and trauma studies. He also holds an MFA from Ohio State University. His nonfiction, poetry, short fiction, and translations have appeared in *Another Chicago Magazine*, *Harvard Review*, *Indiana Review*, *The Literary Review*, *The Los Angeles Review*, *New York Quarterly*, *Prairie Schooner*, *A Public Space*, and *Subtropics*, among others. He is the author of the fiction collection *From the Crooked Timber* (Press 53, 2011). His novel, *The Doors You Mark Are Your Own* (co-authored with Raul Clement), is forthcoming in early 2015 from Dark House Press, and his book of translation, *Blackbirds in September: Selected Shorter Poems of Jürgen Becker*, is forthcoming from Black Lawrence Press in late 2015.